Old Faithful

Story and Illustrations by Bob Reese

Dominie Press, Inc.

"It's time to go,"
said Barney the buffalo.

2

"Don't be late. It's time to go."

"It's time to see,"
said Bubba the bear.

4

"Don't be late. We'll all be there."

Mickey the moose said,
sniffing the air,

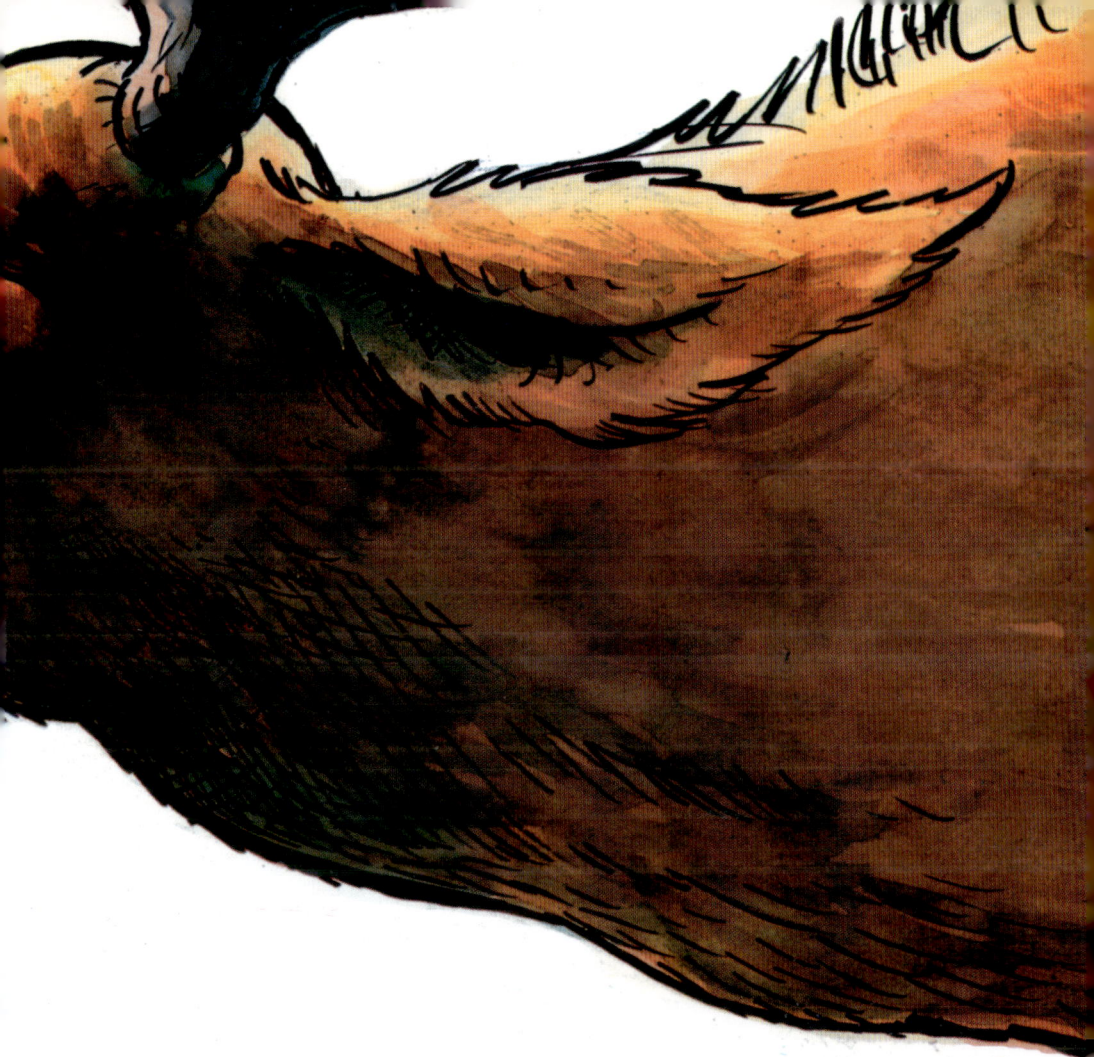

"Don't be late. We'll all be there."

8

Bubba the bear said,
"We'll see Old Faithful when it goes.
Every hour, it really blows."

Barney the buffalo said,
"It's time to see."

Barney ran behind a tree!

Bubba the bear said,
"It's time to see."

Bubba ran behind a tree!

Mickey the moose said,
"It won't scare me.

I won't run behind a tree."

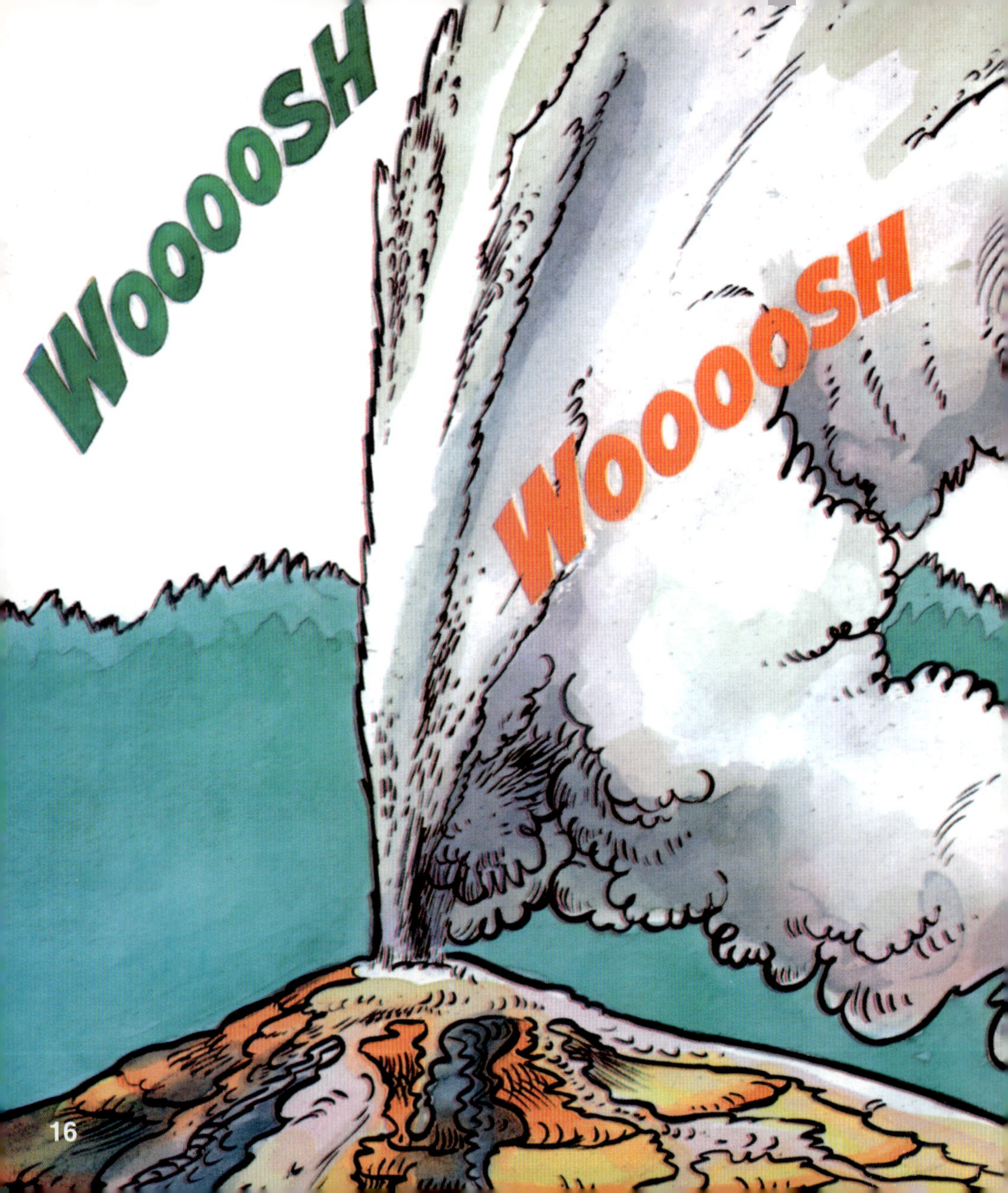
WOOOOSH
WOOOOSH

Old Faithful is big. It really goes.

Every hour, it really blows!

Mickey the moose said,
"It won't scare me."

Then Mickey the moose
ran behind a tree!

I am a
Forty-Word Book

My forty words are:

a	me
air	Mickey
all	moose
Barney	Old
be	ran
bear	really
behind	run
big	said
blows	scare
Bubba	see
buffalo	sniffing
Don't	the
Every	Then
Faithful	there
go (goes)	time
hour	to
I	tree
is	We'll
it (It's)	when
late	won't

Copyright © 2005 Dominie Press, Inc.

Published by:

🐚 **Dominie Press, Inc.**

1949 Kellogg Avenue
Carlsbad, California 92008 USA

www.dominie.com
ISBN 0-7685-2236-6
Printed in Singapore by PH Productions Pte Ltd
1 2 3 4 5 PH 07 06 05